# 4 Steps To a Beautiful Groom

by: Jun S. Yun

Special Thanks:

To my beautiful and supportive wife, Kimberly: Thank you so much for always being there for me during the tough times. Without your encouragement and belief in me, I would not be the man I am today. Thank you for loving me.

Heather Beck: Thank you so much for taking the leap of faith and believing in me. You have not only invested your time and money to help me and my family, but you generously opened up your home to us so that we would have a place to live while getting settled in a new state where we had no one else who could have given us any support. Thank you for believing in me, and for supporting my dream of creating awareness on the importance of proper dog grooming. You truly are a special person, and I will never forget your generosity.

Michelle Knowles, CMG: Thank you for being such a great friend and mentor to me. I will always cherish the time I was fortunate enough to spend with you at Animal Health Services in Cave Creek, AZ. You are such an inspiration to me, and such a wonderful teacher. Thank you for being so generous with your knowledge and sharing your experiences with me. I learned so much from both your written material and by your living example.

Pamela Lauritzen: Thank you so much for dedicating your life to educating groomers on the proper treatment and care of the canine skin and coat. Your life is an example of passion and dedication. I will always be grateful for the information I learned from the ISCC (International Society of Canine Cosmetologists).

Cesar Millan: Thank you so much for the example you have set for me by your life. I would not be where I am today if it was not for the inspiration you have given me through your life experiences and the philosophy you share in your material. I hope to meet you in person one day to personally thank you for the tremendous impact you have made on my life. Because of you, I am the Dog Groomer!

Table of Contents:

Dog grooming is not about making dogs look pretty. That's a nice side effect of properly grooming a dog, but that's not why we do it. We groom our dogs to keep them in good health, and to keep their oils evenly distributed all throughout their coat. This applies to all breeds, and all coat types. They must be brushed regularly. It is not a luxury. Tasty treats and trips to the dog park are a luxury. Regular grooming is a necessity. It requires our time and our effort. Grooming is "Love in Action." Nature has provided a way for us to show our dogs in a very clear and obvious way that we care about them. We are telling them that we love them in a way that they will clearly understand. By brushing them regularly, and keeping their skin feeling good, we are repaying them for all that they do for us. We must work with Mother Nature, and Nature requires our time and effort. My dream is to create awareness on the importance of properly grooming our dogs. Rather than think, "My dog smells, I should wash him," we can instead think to ourselves, "My dog smells, I have to brush him."

I am feeling so grateful that I persevered through many hardships and obstacles in order to become a skilled dog groomer. As a result of years of countless hours of study and application, I have developed my own personal philosophy on dog grooming that I am eager to share with you. There have been so many tests and challenges throughout the years that made me think about quitting on more than one occasion. Because I didn't give in to my fears, or the temptation to take a less challenging path, I am now able to help thousands of people all over the world by sharing my experiences. I am so happy that so many people find the YouTube videos that my wife and I created helpful. Thousands of people have written us to tell us how much we have helped them in their personal grooming experiences.

It's amazes me, and to think that I was tempted to quit so many times. It was not just from my own self-doubts but from others' as well. If you have a passion and a dream that you are pursuing, please don't give up. No matter how hard the situation. No matter what others may think or say. Please continue to do your best and let nothing stop you in the pursuit of happiness.

My intention for writing this book is to simplify the grooming process into 4 simple steps that will be easy to understand. In my previous book, The Art of Grooming, I shared my philosophy on dog grooming and explained the "Why." This book is the next step to the Art of Grooming, where I will explain the "How." If we only realized how important it was to follow each of the steps I will outline in this book, and how much it would benefit the lives of the dogs, I believe that everyone would consider following these 4 simple steps. It is important to understand that "simple" does not always mean "easy." The steps that I will explain in this book will be easy to understand, but it will take time and effort to apply the knowledge. "Knowing is not enough, you must apply; willing is not enough, you must do" Bruce Lee.

I believe that with my experience as a passionate dog groomer - looking closely at every square inch of the dog's skin everyday - I can help a lot of people with what I've learned through personal research and hands-on experience over the years. Thank you so much for taking the time to read this book. By doing so you are making a great investment in the health and comfort of your dog. I believe the information that I will share with you will greatly increase the quality of life for both you and your dogs. We can change the world together, one dog at a time.

# Chapter 1: The Importance of the Process

"Everything has beauty, but not everyone sees it." - Confucius

The more I learn about dog grooming, the more I am convinced that I'll never master the Art of Grooming. Grooming is my art form. I practice it daily, and wholeheartedly. I am an artist and I'm so proud to be a dog groomer. I met another artist who works with me at K9-Lifeline in Draper, Utah (http://www.k9lifeline.net). Her name is Danielle Wiley.

After grooming Danielle's dogs for her I received an amazingly generous tip from her that honestly made me feel uncomfortable. The second time around I refused to accept it! She looked me in the eyes and said something that really made an impact on me. She said, "I want you to have it. It's worth it to me," and I could tell that she meant it. My heart swelled. I felt so appreciated and valued at that moment, and I'll never forget it. I knew at that moment I was in the presence of fellow Jedi Master. You should see her with a half-dozen dogs on leashes walking smoothly around the center. The Force is Strong with this one.

It turns out that she is a passionate baker, and a member of the ABA (American Bakers Association). "Baking is an art," she told me. "There's a science to it." She explained that the ingredients don't get mixed in all at once. There is a process that needs to be followed or the bread won't turn out right. The yeast can't come in contact with the preservatives or the preservatives will kill the yeast. I gained so much from this conversation with Danielle about the Art of Baking. It really is an art form and every loaf is an expression of the baker's heart.

I asked her, "If the baking time and temperature was set properly, putting the bread in the oven and letting it bake is the easy part, right?" She answered, "Yes. Everything is in the prep."

I only asked to emphasize a point that I always like to make. When grooming a dog, if the prep and bath is done properly, the haircut and styling session is the easy part. When we do a proper job grooming the dog, all the body parts flow and connect, making the dog look like a beautifully balanced work of art. The lasting results will be felt by the dog and the owners to enjoy. By the work of our own hands, we can create memories of joy and happiness for the families we serve that will last a lifetime. This is what makes us artists. We are creators. Just like when a baker bakes a delicious loaf of bread for a hungry family to enjoy.

The process is so important, and without following a good process we can never get consistent results. By following the four steps that I will outline in the following chapters, you will be able to achieve the same excellent results that I am able to provide for my clients. Even if another groomer used the same products and tools that I use, they will never be able to produce the same quality results that I do unless they follow the same process. It would be like taking my favorite loaf of bread off the shelf at the grocery store and buying all the ingredients on the back. Then take the ingredients home, mix them all together and put the doughy mess in the oven expecting to get the same loaf of bread that I buy at the store. Even though I used the same ingredients that the bakers did, it wouldn't turn out the same because I did not follow the same process. My 4-Step process is like a recipe for a delicious loaf of bread. There is a science to it, and it must be followed in order to get the same results that my clients enjoy.

My goal is to explain the steps in a clear and simple manner that will make sense to you as you read the following chapters. My sincere hope is that it helps enrich the relationship you have with your dogs. I know that by helping your dogs maintain a healthy skin and coat, it will increase the quality of their lives. They will not only look great, but they will also be able to live comfortably in their own skin. Grooming is hygiene, and by maintaining good hygiene you will prevent a lot of health issues that can cause our dogs a lot of pain and discomfort. The rewards will be a healthy, happy dog that loves you deeply for all the effort you put in to help them live the best life possible.

## Chapter 2: Build Rapport (Step 1)

"Man masters nature not by force, but by understanding"□— Jacob Bronowski

When it comes to dog grooming, many people think that it is just another errand they have to run every month or two by dropping their dog off at a grooming shop. When I watch how animals groom themselves, and each other, I'm reminded that Nature looks at grooming very differently. Grooming is about health and hygiene, and maintaining good hygiene is a daily responsibility. We like to think that grooming a dog is about making them look pretty. But in Nature, grooming is about maintaining a healthy protective barrier in order to survive. It's about health, not vanity.

Animals groom themselves as a way to stay healthy, but also groom each other as a way to establish and strengthen bonds. It is an intimate activity that requires mutual trust, respect and love. This is why I believe it is so important to spend as much time as it takes to get a dog comfortable with me before I begin grooming him. Can you imagine what would happen if a dog walked up to another dog it didn't know and began grooming him? It would most likely cause a fight. My daughters are a great example. I can run my fingers through my daughters' hair, but what if a stranger tried to do that? But what if that stranger spent a week with them doing fun activities and playing together? Then it wouldn't be so weird if he ran his fingers through their hair. My point is that a relationship must be established before another grown man tries to run his fingers through their hair. Just like a relationship must be established before we start brushing a dog we've never met before.

The way I approach a dog depends on the individual dog, and what their body language is telling me. I like to compare the first groom to a first date.

On a first date we usually engage in some light conversation first, and try to keep it interesting. We want to take things slow at first in order to give them a pleasant experience. Then maybe ask for a little more on the second date. Had I tried to jump my wife's pants on our first date, we probably wouldn't be married - and knowing her, I probably would've gone to jail! Now fast forward to being married almost 9 years. I still can't jump her pants whenever I want but at least I won't go to jail for trying. It's the same thing with grooming. The more rapport you have with a dog, the more you can ask of them. When a dog trusts you, respects you, and loves you, they are willing to do almost anything you ask of them.

I believe grooming to be the ultimate dog experience because it is a very intimate experience that helps strengthen the relationship between dog and owner. When else are you going to be that close to your dog for an extended amount of time? Sure we all spend time touching our dogs in intimate and/or sensitive areas when we cuddle with them, but how long does that usually last? Thirty minutes? An hour? The average full groom - meaning a full body haircut - usually lasts about two to three hours start to finish. Keep in mind that if it is your first time grooming a dog it can take all day. I always advise people not to try grooming a dog if they are feeling rushed, nervous or anxious. Dogs do not care about your schedule or where you have to be in an hour. So it's best to make sure you have a clear schedule and few distractions. Grooming a dog properly is one of the most intimate moments you will ever have with your dog, and it will earn you his/her trust, respect and love. When we understand how our dogs view grooming, we understand why it is best not to rush it.

According to Cesar Millan, my personal hero, the three main ingredients to a healthy relationship with our dogs are trust, respect and love. So how does grooming your dog accomplish this? You are helping your dog through a very unnatural experience by giving him leadership, encouragement, direction and guiding him through an experience that can be very frightening.

Think about it from a dog's perspective. A dog's idea of a groom would be to rub it's neck and/or back on some grass, mud, trees, or even worse on the remnants of a dead animal! The nails would naturally file down as they travel, dig, and hunt for food. Our idea of a groom includes water jets, shampoos and conditioners, high-velocity air dryers, clippers, shears, brushes, etc. All of this can be a bit overwhelming to a dog getting groomed professionally for the first time. The most rewarding part of my job as a groomer is to be the one that is there to provide comfort, encouragement and support.

Dogs need us to provide direction and leadership throughout the grooming experience. This builds trust and respect from your dog, and there is nothing more rewarding than earning a dog's trust and respect. The last ingredient is love, and that just comes naturally after you have earned their trust and respect. Now that your dog's face doesn't smell like a dirty gym sock it is much more pleasing to get up close with hugs and kisses! Having a clean, fresh smelling dog encourages the owner to share physical affection with their dog. That closeness, intimacy, helps promote the emotions of love. Dogs are noble creatures and have too much integrity to sell out or be bribed. The only way to earn a dog's trust, respect and love is to be genuine.

# Chapter 3: Prepare the Skin for the Bath (Step 2)

There is so much more to bathing a dog than just throwing them in a tub and lathering them up with shampoo. The dog's skin is a living system, and we should be aware of what is happening at a cellular level before we start interfering. It is our responsibility to gather the right information and apply it in order to help our pets enjoy the best quality of life we can possibly give them. When we groom our dogs, we are engaging in a "Labor of Love." Without us Love would have no other way of expressing itself in a way that provides our dogs with comfort and health. With our hands we can create comfort and happiness for our companions. We are dog groomers. We truly are artists!

I believe that the best way to wash a dog is to begin with a thorough brushing. If you are washing a dog with a short coat, a rubber curry brush and a slicker brush will work well. Dogs with medium coats and long coats will need a thorough combing as well with a metal comb. I like to use greyhound combs and coat kings to help comb out the bundles of dead hairs. Dander and cellular debris that was building up inside the skin also come out along with the dead hairs. This helps clear the pores so that the shampoo and conditioner have room to properly clean and condition the skin.

"Brushing and combing before the bath has three purposes. First, it loosens dirt and dander, and foreign matter. Second; it removes hair shed. Third, it stimulates the skin and allows natural hair oils to circulate... Initial brushing and combing (and de-matting as necessary) is usually done before the bath. Dogs freed of undercoat before their bath are more quickly bathed. Also, the advantages of a bath are greater without undercoat because shampoo, conditioner and rinse water is reaches through the coat down to skin far more easily."
http://www.petgroomer.com/grooming101/articles/brushing_combing-revised.htm

The following quote is from an article in the Grooming Business Magazine titled, The Science of Skin by Christina Pawlosky:

"When groomers are bathing, they must consider the fact that the skin is the largest organ on the dog's body. They must also remind themselves that they are the caretakers of this organ. Groomers have contact with the skin of a pet more than even a veterinarian does, in most cases.

Being the keeper of a dog's skin is an important job. The skin is the front line of the dog's defense system, and often, it displays the first indicator when something is not functioning well internally. When the skin does not look normal, groomers need to share what they see with the owner and recommend a veterinarian visit for a proper diagnosis. However, on the flip side, they need to understand how the skin works so that they are not adding or causing issues for the pet...

Remember, any stimulus can speed up the cellular response and glandular production, whether chemical or mechanical. So, be gentle." http://www.groomingbusiness.com/content/science-skin

According to Pam Lauritzen, founder of the International Society of Canine Cosmetologists (ISCC; www.petstylist.com), the normal skin cycle speeds up when it is disrupted on a cellular level either by washing or clipping the surface of the skin. "It should be noted that when conditioning damaged skin, it must be given at least 2-4 weeks restoration time." ISCC Certification Study Guide; Section 1, page 2. On a cellular level, the skin interprets a bath as an attack on the skin's surface.

Other than a major hurricane or typhoon, when else would a dog's skin be subjected to that kind of treatment? By washing a dog too frequently, we are constantly attacking the skin on a cellular level. When we do this, the skin is never able to function normally because it will always be in a constant state of repair. As soon as it comes out of the recovery mode, it is thrown right back into a state of emergency due to another attack.

"Anything that disrupts the normal functioning of the skin, strips the dog of its protective covering, leaving it vulnerable to its environment. While topical conditioning to restore the surface conditions of the skin may be necessary, it must be recognized that treating the symptoms while neglecting the cause is only half of the solution." ISCC Certification Study Guide; Section 1, page 4. If you are interested in grooming professionally, or would like to learn more in order to groom your own dogs, I highly recommend joining the ISCC (www.petstylist.com).

I've come to believe that it is best to wash our dogs no more than once a month. Rather than washing frequently, I believe it is much better to brush them thoroughly on a regular basis.What I am suggesting is that we research and study the anatomy of the dog's skin and coat thoroughly before going in there and interfering with the natural flora. There are mites, bacteria, fungus and other cellular debris that live on the dog's skin, and they all balance each other out. It's a lot like a rainforest in there with it's own ecosystem.

When we start to interfere with the natural flora without knowing what we are doing and why we are doing it, we unknowingly cause the system to get thrown off balance. Because it is all happening on a cellular level, we never see the effects immediately. It's usually a few days or weeks after the bath that we begin to see the symptoms, and most people will blame the diet.

Diet does play a role in skin health, but that would be like changing my diet to try to heal athlete's foot. It wouldn't hurt, but it probably wouldn't help much either.

I like to think of the skin as the Hair Factory because that's basically what it is. It produces oils and helps protect the internal organs, but to put it simply, the skin is what produces the hair. It is not a clean coat that helps the skin maintain a healthy flora, but rather a healthy skin that produces beautiful smooth hair. So just like any factory, if the product it produces is faulty, it is best to focus on the factory rather than the product. If a factory that makes dog treats, for example, produces bad treats, it would be best to dump the products and fix whatever is going on at the factory so it can make better treats. We wouldn't try to collect all the bad treats and clean them up in order to repackage and resell them. That would be ridiculous, and would permanently ruin the company's reputation. The same could be said about dogs with bad coats. Rather than try to save the hair, clean it up and make it smell nice (for a few days), it would be much better to get rid of the dull coat and focus on the skin so it can produce better hair.

I personally believe it is better to pull the hairs out rather than shave them. If we simply shave the coat off, we leave the dull, brittle hairs inside the skin. That means that the hair that grows out will still be dull and brittle because it is still inside the pores, and will continue to grow. A dog's skin that grows a medium length, double-coat may not continue to grow that hair, but it would cause the pores to get backed up.

Over time it will cause irritation and bumps, which can lead to more serious problems down the road. When we focus on clearing the pores out and giving the skin a healthy environment to breathe and grow fresh new hairs, we don't have to worry about the coat. Take care of the skin and let the skin take care of the coat. Rather than focus on the product, focus on the factory. When the factory is running well it will produce good quality products. I believe that my responsibility as a groomer is to take care of the skin first, and give a good haircut second. Good grooming is simply, good skin care.

## Chapter 4: Shampoo and Conditioner (Step 3)

Did you know that the more often we wash our dogs, the more likely it is that they will produce a stronger odor? Or that Baby Shampoo is not safe to use on dogs? I'd like to share what I've learned during my career to help owners have dogs with beautiful, problem-free coats.

The following is from an article on PetMD.com titled, Maintaining Your Dog's Skin pH:

"Depending on breed, gender, climate, and the anatomical size on the dog, the pH levels range from 5.5 to 7.5, tending toward a more alkaline concentration. Therefore, if a shampoo that is formulated for human skin is used on a dog, the dog's acid mantle *(This is a lightly acidic layer that covers the skin, serving as a barrier to protect the porous topmost layer of the skin, the stratum corneum, from environmental contaminants such as bacteria and viruses.)* will be disrupted, creating an environment where bacteria, parasites, and viruses can run rampant. Unknowingly, many pet owners will repeat washings of their dogs because of the smell caused by a proliferation of bacteria, making the problem worse as the skin's acid mantle/pH level becomes more imbalanced. Additionally, if the shampoo makes the skin feel dry, your dog will scratch at its skin, creating abrasions for bacteria to invade. It quickly becomes a vicious cycle...

Just as you would look for a shampoo that helps maintain the pH balance of your own scalp, you should also concentrate on finding a shampoo with a pH balance that is specifically balanced for a dog's skin. Dog shampoos should be in the neutral range, around 7. Many shampoo manufacturers will include the pH level on the label, but at the very least, they will clearly state that the shampoo is pH-balanced for dogs."

To read the entire article, which I highly recommend, please follow the link: http://www.petmd.com/dog/grooming/evr_dg_shampoo_for_dogs

I used to tell people that it was ok to use Dawn dish detergent as a degreaser because they are used to wash the ducks in oil spills. This could not be further from the truth. I asked Pam Lauritzen, founder of the International Society of Canine Cosmetologists (ISCC, www.petsylist.com), whether it was ok for us to use Dawn. She replied that the ducks in the commercials are in a life or death situation and they need to get the toxic oil off of them immediately. Once those ducks are cleaned and they are no longer at risk of dying, they can treat the skin for the damages caused by the oil and the dish detergent. Dogs coming in for a bath and a haircut are not in a life or death situation. We should not be using Dawn because it is too harsh on the dog's skin. The pH is not right for the dog, and pH is everything.

I asked Michelle Knowles, CMG and Certified Skin Aesthetician, whether or not it was ok for us to use Dawn on dogs as a degreaser to hear her thoughts. She told me that using Dawn is very harmful to the dog's skin, and because it is so drying it is imperative that we follow up the rinse with a good conditioner. We should also add oils to replace what was stripped out by the Dawn. She said that they should be adding conditioner and nourishing oils like Argan Oil, Advocado Oil or Emu Oil back into the skin and coat after they wash them in Dawn. If you are interested in learning more, or becoming certified as a skin care specialist, I highly recommend her educational programs. The information to her training modules can be found at this link: http://www.ivsanbernardus.com/home-main/pet-aesthetician-certification-program/.

It was Michelle who taught me the importance of always using conditioner after the shampoo. Even curly coats like Bichons and Poodles need conditioner after the shampoo. Early in my career I was taught that the conditioner causes the hair to lay flat and prevents it from drying fluffy and straight. Michelle showed me that what I had been taught was untrue, and also unhealthy for the dog's skin. She also explained to me how the shampoo works on a microscopic level. Shampoo opens up the hair fibers like a pinecone and attaches itself to the dirt particles and grease. This is why it is so important to let the shampoo sit for at least 5 minutes, in order to give it time to make the necessary chemical reactions. It is not our hands scrubbing the dog that does the cleaning, but rather the shampoo as long as we give it the time it needs to do it's job. When we rinse the shampoo off, that's when the cleaning happens. As we wash away the shampoo, the dirt and grease it has attached itself to are all washed away as well. If we just leave the hair open and dry the dog off without using conditioner, we are leaving the hair open to dirt and bacteria. By applying conditioner the hair fibers fill up with moisture, which seals them shut and also provides a protective layer of oil to repel the dirt and bacteria.

"Do you ever wonder why your pet starts to smell bad 1 or 2 days after a bath? This usually means that the natural oils that were shampooed away were not replaced by a conditioner and the sebaceous glands are overproducing to try to protect the delicate skin. This is the reason it is always best to use a conditioner or balsam after shampooing, then after the dog is dry, rub a small amount of oil into the coat and 'polish' with the bristle brush. This will keep the glands in the skin from overreacting and the dog will smell nice for an extended period of time." (www.isbusa.com) Michelle Knowles, 2012 Copyright C&K Distributing, LLC

When bathing your dogs at home, I have a few rules that will help you achieve excellent results.

1) Card the coat before washing to help clear the pores of the built up undercoat and cellular debris. This will ensure the shampoo and conditioner will have room to clean and condition the skin properly.

2) Always use conditioner to help add moisture and oils back into the skin and help protect the hairs from bacteria. This will help keep your dog smelling good and feeling good for much longer.

3) Brush or comb the coat in the direction it is supposed to lay naturally to help train the hair to lay nicely. This will also help redistribute oils all throughout the coat, and your dog will feel silky soft after the bath.

## Chapter 5: Polish & Protect the Coat (Step 4)

The last step involves drying the coat properly, and sealing the hairs in order to protect the skin and coat. After the final rinse in the tub, I like to use my hands to squeeze out the excess water in the coat. I also encourage the dog to shake because they can get rid of most of the water naturally with just one full body shake. Then I use a clean, dry towel to absorb more of the moisture from the dog's coat. I've learned that it is best to lay the towel down for the dog to stand on while using a high-velocity air drier to catch the moisture being blown off of the dog. That way a lot of the moisture is absorbed by the towel rather than floating around in the air, which causes the drying session to take even longer.

When using the high-velocity (HV) air drier, I always work from the back of the dog to the front. This is because if you take the nozzle from the HV drier and make a straight line on the dog's body moving from the front of the dog to the back, you will notice that it leaves a trail of whipped and wavy hair that causes cow licks. However, when you do the same thing but move from the back to the front of the dog, it lays the hair nice and flat in the direction it should lay naturally. That's the only reason I work from the back of the dog towards the front, and from the feet up to the body. It just lays the hair nicely in the direction it should naturally lay. "Everything we do should be with the end goal in mind." Christina Pawlosky, CMG.

If you do not have a HV drier, than you can use a regular hand-held blow drier like the kind we use for our own hair. Just be careful not to use too much heat because it can damage their skin. I like to use the Cool or Warm setting rather than the Hot. Be sure to keep moving along the dog's body and not spend too much time on one area when using a blow drier. You can always go back and work on an area that is still damp.

Some dogs will not tolerate being dried artificially and will react negatively to any type of drier. In these cases, I like to comb or brush the coat in the direction that the hair lays naturally which is called "setting the coat." Once the coat is brushed down so that the hair lies nicely, I allow the coat to air dry for about an hour or two before brushing the coat again until it is dry. It is very important to allow the dog to shake and thoroughly dry them with a towel before setting the coat. It is not a good idea to keep a dog too wet because the coat will take much longer to dry, and it increases the chance of the dog getting too cold.

After the dog is dry, I like to spray a leave in conditioner on the coat and brush it into the coat with a slicker brush or a metal comb. My personal favorites are Envirogroom's finishing sprays, or a product called The Stuff for Dogs. By spraying a conditioning spray, it not only gives them a pleasant smell, but it gives the coat a soft, silky finish. After applying a coat conditioner of your choice, use a natural bristle brush to brush the entire coat from head to tail. Always brush with the grain, not against the grain in order to continually train the hair to lie nicely. I personally like to use a horsehair bristle brush, but a boar's bristle brush is great to use as well. By using a natural bristle brush, the bristles will catch the oils and distribute them evenly throughout the dog's coat. This will form a protective barrier that will repel dust, debris, and unwanted moisture such as urine or dirty water. This final step will ensure that your dog will stay clean and smell nice for several weeks after the bath. Depending on the individual dog's lifestyle, it can even last for months after the bath.

These are the 4 Steps to a Beautiful Groom. My intention is to make sure each step makes sense and is easy to understand. In the next few chapters I will explain how to apply these simple steps to any dog you groom no matter what the circumstances may be. Sometimes we may encounter an exceptionally fearful or aggressive dog that is challenging to work with. Many people have asked me, "How do I brush a dog that will not allow me to brush him?" Or, "What if my dog freaks out when I try to clip his nails or brush his face?" I have come up with a philosophy that I hope will help you understand how to deal with challenging situations during the grooming process. I call it the 3 C's of Grooming: Calm, Confident and Compassionate.

# Chapter 6: The 3 C's of Grooming - Calm

I believe that to be an excellent dog groomer there are 3 characteristics that a person must practice and develop into their character. I'm going share these ideas that I've been thinking about for quite some time now. I've even considered writing a separate book about it, but I think it's best to keep things short and simple so I've decided to include them in this book. I call them the 3 C's of Dog Grooming.

The first C stands for Calm. In the Merriam-Webster dictionary, Calm is defined as

: a quiet and peaceful state or condition

: a peaceful mental or emotional state.

I believe that another way to look at being calm is to be mindful, or awareness. It is to be mindful of the moment and completely aware of how you're feeling. When we are calm, the dogs can feel it and this allows them to be calm as well. But we can't fake it. Once I had a lady bring me her vicious little Toy Poodle named Diva. She said that no groomer has ever been able to finish her, and she always ends up looking horrible because they can't finish the groom. Little Diva was a hot mess. Her mother stayed and watched the entire groom, and said that she's been looking her whole life for a groomer like me. She couldn't believe how calm I was while her little Diva was screaming and biting me. The trick is to breathe deep through the belly rather than the chest, and fight off any feelings of fear or anxiety. When we breathe deeply with our belly rather than our chest, it resets our physical state and helps our body to calm down.

Cesar Millan is one of my favorite mentors, and I watched several episodes of the Dog Whisperer where he would just allow the dog to bite him. He wouldn't pull his hand back, but instead he would leave his hand exactly where it was. He explains that if he pulls away in fear, than the dog will no longer trust or respect him because by his actions he has shown the dog that he no longer trusts him. By not pulling away, but rather staying calm, the dog doesn't bite down hard and understands that his hand is supposed to be there. By his actions he shows the dog that he trusts him not to harm him, so the dog in return trusts that Cesar's touch will not harm him either. It's amazing to watch, but even more amazing to actually experience. I explained this to Diva's mom as she watched in amazement. Diva never bit down too hard, and when she would bite a bit harder than I'm comfortable with I would correct her with one of Cesar's trademark "Tssst."

Being calm comes from self-confidence, and self-confidence comes from self-respect. I'm paraphrasing, but I heard that in one of Brian Tracy's motivational speeches and I liked it a lot. I am able to be calm when a Scottish Terrier wants to snap my hand off, because I am confident in my abilities. I am confident in my abilities because I spent countless hours practicing my scissor skills, and clipper control. I've worked through the muscle cramps, the achy joints and sore muscles. I've been bit too many times to even try to keep count. There is no substitute for hard work and the experience that it brings. It builds self-respect, knowing that you put in your best effort. That self-respect builds self-confidence, and having that confidence in myself gives me the ability to stay calm no matter what the circumstances. It takes practice, and I still have times where I feel myself panic under the pressures of the day. That's when I have to remind myself to be mindful of the moment and how I am feeling. I take a deep breath in and visualize my muscles relaxing as I breathe out.

Every time I remind myself to take a deep breath, the dogs seem to notice the physical change in my body and they calm down as well.

It takes courage to be calm rather than give into our fears. I know when business slows down we tend to panic, and some people start sending out coupons and discounts in desperation. All businesses and industries have their trends, ups-and-downs, and cycles. When it slows down, don't panic. Do some deep cleaning that may have gone neglected while things were busy. Work on some other projects that will help the business. Or have a brainstorming session to bring in new ideas. When we do our best, and we know that the work we do is good, than we don't have anything to worry about. Dogs will always need to be groomed, and they all can't go on vacation or die at the same time. Being calm is about focusing on the moment and doing our best with the task, or groom, at hand. Remember, when we are calm the dogs will be calm, but they know us too well to be faked out. We can't fake being calm when we're feeling anxious. The dog will pick up on it immediately. That's why I love working with dogs so much. It keeps me honest with myself. They don't care how many YouTube subscribers I have! They couldn't care less that I've written a book about grooming dogs. All the dog cares about is the energy you represent, as Cesar Millan would put it.

Working with dogs has helped me tremendously with becoming a more calm and honest person. It's easy to trick people and act calm when you are really feeling anxious or nervous, but it's impossible to fool a dog. Dogs are able to pick up on our "biowaves" according to an article called Golden Heroes by Kathy Salzberg in the Groomer to Groomer Magazine.

In the article she explains that the Golden Retrievers that were trained to help war veterans who suffer from PTSD were able to detect changes in their "biowaves." According to the article, biowaves are vibrations that are emitted from our bodies that dogs can sense. When the war vets would start to feel anxiety the vibrations would change and the dogs would be able to respond accordingly. That is why even though we try to act calm, and even convince ourselves that we are being calm, the dogs cannot be fooled. When we are truly calm, the dogs will let us know by becoming calm as well.

# Chapter 7: The 3 C's of Grooming – Confident

The second C I'd like to discuss is "Confidence", and what it means to me to be a confident dog groomer. I believe that it is a crucial component to being an excellent groomer.

The following is the Merriam-Webster online dictionary definition of the word Confidence:

: a feeling or belief that you can do something well or succeed at something

: a feeling or belief that someone or something is good or has the ability to succeed at something

: the feeling of being certain that something will happen or that something is true

"Confidence can be a self-fulfilling prophecy as those without it may fail or not try because they lack it and those with it may succeed because they have it rather than because of an innate ability." https://en.wikipedia.org/wiki/Confidence

It's obvious that having confidence in oneself is a good thing. We can all agree that it is vital to have self-confidence to be good at anything. But how does someone go about attaining a high level of confidence if they do not feel they have much at the moment? It's not like there's a store that sells "Confidence" where we can stock up when we're low. Where does it come from? I believe that self-confidence comes from self-respect, which comes from self-discipline and integrity.

Every time we do the things we know we should be doing (integrity), we start to respect ourselves more (self-respect). It's not always easy to do what we know our higher selves would have us do, and that is the challenge we must be willing to face. That's where the self-discipline comes in. An example of self-discipline is when I make myself do something productive rather than sit and watch TV shows or a movie. One of my favorite mentors is Jim Rohn. He said, "Discipline weighs ounces, regret weighs tons." In order to have true confidence - not the puffed-up version that we call Arrogance - but true confidence that inspires confidence in others, we must have the discipline to do what's right. "Discipline is the bridge between goals and accomplishment," Jim Rohn. When we consistently do our very best in everything that is asked of us, we will develop a high level of respect for ourselves. The outcome is self-confidence.

We've all heard that Courage is not the absence of Fear, but the ability to act in spite of fear. I believe the same can be said of Confidence. It is not the absence of Doubt and Insecurities, but the ability to take inspired action in spite of them. Over the course of 5 years, I've been through more ups and downs than a roller coaster at Six Flags! One day my wife and I are giving each other high-fives, and another we're digging through the change in our cash register to buy gas. There have been times where we would take our daughters to the community garden in Chamblee, and they would water the plants while my wife and I would pick veggies to make dinner with. Even when we had just a couple of lawn chairs as furniture and slept on warped floors, we never let ourselves get down. To someone looking at my life now, it would be easy to say that I'm lucky. I suppose I am very lucky and blessed. But it took years of pulling myself back out of the gutter.

There were so many times that I wanted to walk away from this industry - especially when I knew that I could make a more secure paycheck doing something else. My family and close friends would also try to talk me into another career. There were too many nights where I would look up at the stars for answers while my wife and daughters were asleep. Sometimes things just seemed hopeless. I believe it was an inner confidence I had that kept me going. Just like Merriam-Webster describes, it was "a feeling or belief that someone or something is good or has the ability to succeed at something."

Confidence comes from knowing that you did your very best every day, with every task. No matter how insignificant the task may seem, it all matters in the end. Jim Rohn describes two kinds of philosophies that will determine where you will end up in life. The first says, "If this is all they pay, I'm not coming in early and I'm not staying late." That's one philosophy to live by. The other is, "No matter what they pay, I'm going to give it my all." That's the philosophy of a confident person. He says, "Always do more than what you're paid to do in order to make an investment in your own future." Brian Tracy says it another way: "Always go the extra mile. You'll never find any traffic there." It's not about being the best at anything. It's about doing your best at everything. Trying to be the best will make you arrogant. Working each day to do your very best will make your confident. Why should we do our very best, especially when a Shih Tzu owner complains about the price? We do our best because that is the purpose of our lives. "Every life form seems to strive to its maximum except human beings. How tall will a tree grow? As tall as it possibly can. Human beings, on the other hand, have been given the dignity of choice. You can choose to be all or you can choose to be less. Why not stretch up to the full measure of the challenge and see what all you can do?" Jim Rohn

To sum things up, if you want to be more confident you must start by having integrity. It takes discipline to develop a habit of doing what we believe is right. Once we develop the habit of integrity through practicing self-discipline, we will have respect for ourselves. This is the recipe for Self-Confidence: Integrity gives birth to Self-Respect. Self-Respect builds Self-Confidence. The more we repeat this process on a daily basis, the higher our level of confidence. Why is it so important to be confident? Because the clients will respect you more, and the dogs will be much more willing to cooperate with you. Imagine a dentist that is very friendly and nice, but is also very timid and has shaky hands. No matter how nice he is, if his trembling hands approach my mouth with those sharp tools I'm not sticking around! Let's imagine that another dentist is not so friendly, but he is calm and confident. I'm much more likely to put my trust in him.

To end this chapter, I'd like to share my Journal entry from May 26th, 2014:

"I reminded them that we all have a purpose & we are all capable of GREATNESS - actually we're meant for GREATNESS! That is our purpose - is to realize our own unique greatness - our unique special powers. No two superheroes are alike - they are all unique with unique abilities. They don't envy each other & even if two heroes have the same ability it is never exactly the same. The way each hero uses the ability & the unique combination of other talents and abilities makes it uniquely their own. We are like brainwashed heroes who go on each day never knowing who we really are or what our real purpose is. We never realize our full potential before we die. That is what should really scare us - not dying, but dying without ever knowing why we lived. What is my special power? I have so many abilities and talents - I should do whatever I can do with all my might."

# Chapter 8: The 3 C's of Grooming – Compassion

This is the final component to The 3 C's of Grooming: Calm, Confident and Compassionate. So far I've discussed why I believe that being calm and confident is an absolute must in order to groom dogs successfully. I also shared where I believe these two qualities come from, and how we can obtain them. In this chapter I will discuss the last piece of the puzzle, which is Compassion.

The Merriam Webster dictionary defines compassion as:

: a feeling of wanting to help someone who is sick, hungry, in trouble, etc.

: pity for and a desire to help someone

I wholeheartedly agree with the first definition, but I have a hard time accepting that compassion is a feeling of "pity for" someone. The word "pity" usually implies that we feel sorry for someone; meaning that we feel that we are somehow above that person. This is not compassion, in my opinion. Compassion says, like the English Reformer, John Bradford, "But for the grace of God, there go I." It is the ability to understand that we are all suffering in some way, and that we are all connected through those experiences. I love Cesar Millan, if you haven't noticed from my writing and my YouTube videos. One of the best lines I've heard him say is, "You can never help anyone that you feel sorry for. If you want to help somebody, you cannot allow yourself to feel sorry for them."

That episode of the Dog Whisperer was life changing for me. I realized that I often do feel sorry for the dogs that I groom, and that negative energy does not help the dog. In order to help the dogs in my care, I must see them as no less than me. We both experience pain, fear and sadness. Rather than feel pity, I should feel connected. I used to think, "I have to help you because you're such a mess." I now think, "We're going to get through this together because I understand your suffering." Compassion is the ability to care deeply for another because you feel connected with them, not because you pity them.

While living in Chamblee, GA, we had to make trips to the coin laundry several times a week because our washer and dryer broke. On one occasion I took my two girls with me to give my wife some much needed time alone. They were 6 and 3 at the time, and they loved playing with the pool table! I tried teaching them the rules of the game, but they couldn't care less. They would use the pool sticks like hockey sticks and guide the balls into the holes. In just a few moments my 4 quarters were spent, and they'd want to "play" it again. I gave them about 5 dollars worth of quarters and told them that was all they could spend. Then a guy that looked homeless came and started playing with them. I kept a close eye on them just in case, but he seemed genuinely nice. It was so nice to hear them laughing. Even when his shot was interrupted by an unexpected slap shot, he would just laugh and try to shoot another ball into another hole while one of my girls played goalie. We talked later while I folded the clothes, and I realized that his set of circumstances could have happened to anyone. It could've been me standing in his shoes. He told me about his father, a great man with high morals, who he was never able to make proud before he passed. He told me that is name is Robert, after his father, and he wishes he could be half the man his father was. This man had been through a lot of shit, and I truly felt a deep connection with him.

I didn't pity him, or feel sorry for him. He never even asked for any money. He just needed to talk to someone. This was a good guy that had fallen into some tough times. "But for the grace of God, there go I."

One day I was getting off the exit to our house, and there standing on the side of the street was Robert holding a sign that read, "Will work for food. Anything will help. God Bless." I opened my window and called out to him, "Robert! How are you? It's good to see you again!" He immediately hid the sign behind his back, and stammered for words as if he was embarrassed. He said, "My father would roll over in his grave if he knew I was out here doing this. I hate doing this. I hate being out here like this having to beg. I wish I was more like my dad." I felt for this man. My heart went out to him, and I wanted to give him some money but I had none. I, myself, was going through some very difficult times, and I wished that I had something to give him. I immediately realized that I was feeling sorry for him. I shouldn't pity him, just like I wouldn't want anyone to pity me. We were both going through some difficult times, and I was no better than him. I looked him in the eyes, and told him, "Robert, you know all the good qualities about your dad that made him so great? All of those qualities are in you. Everything that made him great, all of it is in you too. You have what it takes to be a great man like your father was, and I'm sure he's proud of you no matter what you do." He nodded, and we looked at each other in a way that words were no longer necessary. I felt compassion for him.

Without the quality of Compassion, grooming dogs can be a very frustrating and difficult experience. Without compassion it is nearly impossible to interact with some unreasonable dog owners. So where does compassion come from? How do we fill up on compassion when we feel low?

I believe that true compassion comes from being compassionate toward ourselves. It takes practice, but try to develop a habit of being kind to yourself. Treat yourself like someone you really love and care about. I used to say things like, "Why am I so useless?" or "Why am I such an idiot?" and "I'm worthless!" I remember telling people, "I know I'm hard on other people, but that's because I'm harder on myself than anyone else." Isn't that the truth? We're often so hard on ourselves, and sometimes we say things to ourselves that we wouldn't even say to someone we dislike.

Something that has helped me tremendously is being able to say, "... but I'm getting better." For example, "Man, I messed up on that Bichon's feet. But I'm getting better at that everyday." Every time I let myself off the hook, I find it easier to let others off the hook as well. I find that when I am kind to myself, it comes out naturally when dealing with others. We cannot give out what we don't have. It is still a practice for me, but I am becoming more aware when I'm feeling upset, embarrassed or frustrated with myself. At those times, I talk to myself the way I would a really good friend that I cared about - or better yet, my daughters. I would never rail into them for making an honest mistake the way I do myself. "Be careful how you talk to yourself because you are always listening." Lisa M Hayes

On my journey to becoming the best dog groomer I can possibly be, I have found that in doing so I have become a better person than I used to be. Dr. Wayne Dyer says that true nobility is not about being better than anyone else. It's about being better than you used to be. I believe that dog grooming provides us with the greatest opportunity to become better each and every day.

The 3 C's of Grooming can be applied to all areas of our lives. Being calm helps us to be more mindful in stressful situations. Being confident means that we respect ourselves for doing the things we know are right. Being compassionate means that we love ourselves so that we can love others. To be an excellent dog groomer means to be an excellent human being. Not perfect, but excellent. A mentor of mine named Ted Woehrle, whom I have the utmost respect for, told me once, "Perfection is unattainable. Excellence is." He explained, "It's always nice to work with excellent people; it's almost impossible to work with a perfectionist." When we expect ourselves to be perfect, we will naturally expect it from others as well. That usually results in frustration with both yourself and others.

Rather than try to be perfect, be kind to yourself and others. By doing so I find that things do work out perfectly. This will make you a compassionate person. I don't think that the 3 C's have to be in any particular order. Being compassionate can help one become more confident, which can help them be calm in stressful situations. Being confident in oneself can help be more compassionate towards others, resulting in a more calm state of mind. Rather than think of the 3 C's as a linear recipe to follow, I think it would be better to view them as interconnected and co-dependent like a triangle.

Thank you so much for taking the time to read this book. I really hope you found this book to be both helpful and enjoyable to read. My intention is to share my thoughts and experiences to help add value to your grooming experiences. Thank you again for your time and attention. I am so grateful for you, and I truly hope that the information that I've shared in this book will be of great value to both you and your dogs.

Made in the USA
San Bernardino, CA
25 February 2019